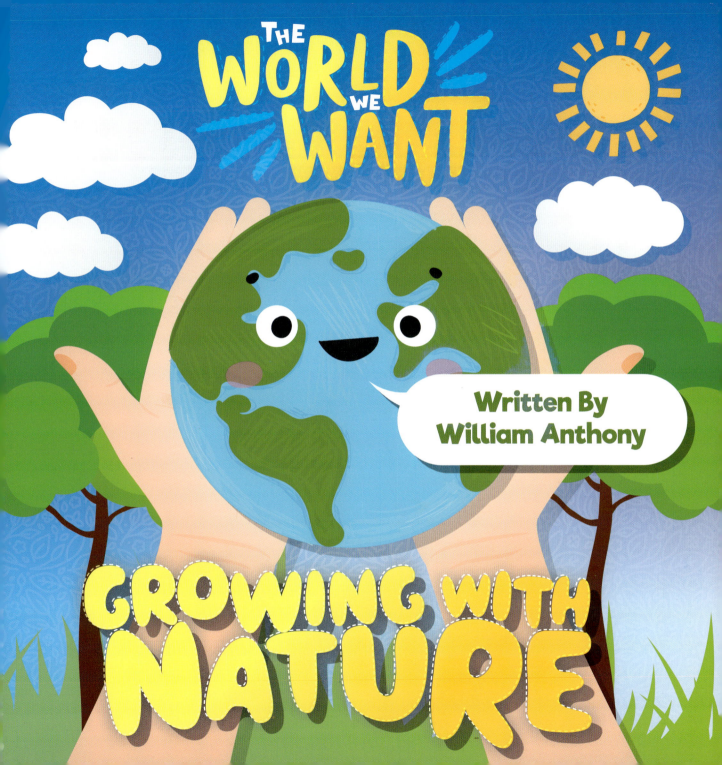

Growing with Nature © 2024 BookLife Publishing
This edition is published by arrangement with BookLife Publishing

sales@northstareditions.com
888-417-0195

Library of Congress Control Number:
2025930769

ISBN
979-8-89359-334-1 (library bound)
979-8-89359-418-8 (paperback)
979-8-89359-388-4 (epub)
979-8-89359-364-8 (hosted ebook)

Printed in the United States of America
Mankato, MN
092025

Written by:
William Anthony

Edited by:
Rebecca Phillips-Bartlett

Designed by:
Rob Delph

American adaptation copyright © 2026 by North Star Editions, Mendota Heights, MN 55120. All rights reserved. No part of this book may be reproduced or utilized in any form or by any means without written permission from the publisher.

All facts, statistics, web addresses and URLs in this book were verified as valid and accurate at time of writing. No responsibility for any changes to external websites or references can be accepted by either the author or publisher.

PHOTO CREDITS

All images are courtesy of Shutterstock.com, unless otherwise specified. Front Cover – Tanarch, cosmaa, Hafid Firman, GoodStudio, venimo, StockSmartStart. 4&5 – D-VISIONS, PeopleImages.com – Yuri A. 6&7 – nnattalli, Elena Elisseeva, Fotokostic, PxB. 8&9 – haireena, Jacob Lund, Andrii Bezvershenko. 10&11 – CherylRamalho, Searra Liggett. 12&13 – Tippman98x, Yamagiwa, Silentgunman, TarikVision. 14&15 – JStandret, Alexwilko, Oksana_Schmidt. 16&17 – NOlga_Ratova, ML Robinson, Elena Chevalier, JurateBuiviene, Oksana_Schmidt, Anna Bova. 18&19 – SeventyFour, ChameleonsEye, RGtimeline. 20&21 – racool_studio, Spalnic, Anton Starikov, Yuri Samsonov, Tatiana Vorona, Anna Svetlova, canvas.mosaic. 22&23 – SolStock (iStockphotos), Frans Blok, Harry Wedzinga, JoannaTkaczuk.

CONTENTS

Page 4   No New Planet
Page 6   Growing
Page 8   Eco-Friendly Growing
Page 10   Rewilding
Page 14   Upcycling for Wildlife
Page 18   Grow Your Own
Page 22   Love Our Planet
Page 24   Glossary and Index

Words that look like <u>this</u> can be found in the glossary on page 24.

NO NEW PLANET

We all live on planet Earth. Earth is home to many different animals and plants. Together, humans, animals, and plants make up our planet's ecosystem.

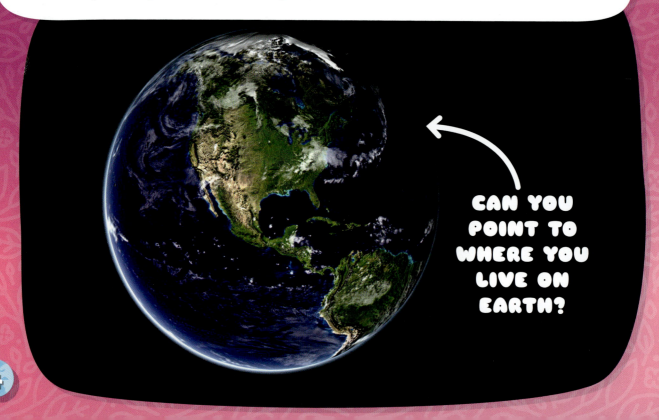

CAN YOU POINT TO WHERE YOU LIVE ON EARTH?

We can't move to a new planet. It's very important to look after Earth so we don't ruin our home. We must look after nature and take care of the environment.

GROWING

People grow plants for lots of reasons. We grow crops to make food, oil, and clothes. We plant trees to make paper or wood. Sometimes, we plant flowers just to make our yards pretty.

Growing plants is important for our daily lives. However, the ways we do it can be harmful to our planet. For example, we sometimes spray crops with things that can hurt wildlife.

Wildlife includes all the wild animals around us.

ECO-FRIENDLY GROWING

If we want to keep Earth healthy, we need to make careful choices when we grow plants. Sustainable growing is when we grow plants in a way that helps the wildlife on our planet.

Some people grow plants to replace ones that have been cut down. Other people grow food at home to <u>reduce</u> the harmful impact of growing crops. There are lots of different ways to grow plants sustainably.

REWILDING

Animals eat plants. They also use plants as their homes. When people make new buildings, they often dig up fields. This means animals lose the plants they need.

Rewilding is one way to give wild spaces back to animals. For example, we can let wildflowers grow in our yards and cut the grass less often.

WILDFLOWERS

Rewilding helps animals such as birds, bugs, and bees to thrive.

Let's rewild part of your yard!

Do you have a grassy yard? Ask your adult if you can rewild part of it. Mow the grass less and plant some _native_ plants.

If you do not have grass, ask if you can plant flowers in some pots.

Rewilding should welcome animals back into your yard. Keep a list of the animals you see!

Before rewilding

Some ants
Snails
Slugs

After rewilding

Lots of ants
Worms
Butterflies
Songbirds
Bees
Owls
Snails
Slugs
A squirrel!

UPCYCLING FOR WILDLIFE

Have you ever visited a forest? If you get the chance, have a close look under some fallen leaves, in a pine cone, or behind some tree bark. You will find lots of bugs living there!

Don't touch any of the animals you see!

We often cut down forests to create space for farms. This means animals lose their homes.

Some people choose to upcycle their garbage to give bugs a new place to live.

Upcycling is when we turn old garbage into something new and useful.

Let's upcycle our garbage into a bug hotel!

1.

Save an old tin can that was used for food. Take the label off and ask an adult to wash it.

2.

Let the can dry. Then, paint the outside with bright colors to <u>attract</u> lots of bugs.

16

3. Ask your adult to take you somewhere to gather old sticks, pine cones, and pieces of tree bark from the ground.

4. Fill your tin can with them. Be careful—the opening of the can might be sharp.

5. Put your bug hotel outside. See which animals are using it after a week.

GROW YOUR OWN

Where do you get your fruit and vegetables? Do you get them from a store? The food in stores goes on a long journey from a farm to the store to your home.

Every journey that a vehicle makes has an impact on our planet. Vehicles are often bad for Earth's temperature and air. It is better to grow food at home to avoid those long journeys.

3.

Add a little water to make the cotton balls damp.

5.

After a week, cut off the tops of the sprouts and try eating them. You could try them on a sandwich!

4.

Sprinkle sprout seeds over the cotton balls. Leave the pot in a warm, sunny place.

LOVE OUR PLANET

What actions will you take to look after our planet?

It is so important to take care of our planet. Growing plants in a way that is safe for our planet is a great start. People are always finding new ways to grow plants.

Whether it is rewilding your yard, upcycling waste into homes for wildlife, or growing food at home, you can help. By looking after nature, we can create the world we want!

REWILDING

HELPING WILDLIFE

HOMEGROWN FOOD

GLOSSARY

ATTRACT	gain something's or someone's interest
CROPS	plants that are grown by farmers
ECOSYSTEM	everything that lives together in an environment
ENVIRONMENT	the surroundings that an animal, plant, or human lives in
NATIVE	originally coming from or growing in a certain area
NATURE	the world around us and everything in it that is not made by humans
REDUCE	make something smaller in size or amount
TEMPERATURE	how hot or cold something is
VEHICLES	machines that are used to carry people or things from one place to another

INDEX

air	19	**food**	6, 9, 16, 18–19, 23	**trees**	6, 14, 17
bugs	11, 14–17			**vehicles**	19
fields	10	**sprouts**	20–21	**yards**	6, 11–13, 23
flowers	6, 11–12	**stores**	18		